IMAGES
of England

CHEADLE
THE SECOND SELECTION

Looking east along High Street in about 1905. The first building on the left is The Old Royal Oak and on the right there are four public houses in view. First is The Royal Oak, then can be seen the iron bracket from which the sign of The Cross Keys Inn would normally hang. At the corner of Cross Street is The Top Bulls Head with The Wheatsheaf Hotel next door to it.

IMAGES
of England

CHEADLE
THE SECOND SELECTION

W. George Short

TEMPUS

First published 1999
Reprinted 2004

Tempus Publishing Limited
The Mill, Brimscombe Port,
Stroud, Gloucestershire, GL5 2QG
www.tempus-publishing.com

British Library Cataloguing in Publication Data.
A catalogue record for this book is available from the British Library.

ISBN 0 7524 1824 6

Typesetting and origination by Tempus Publishing Limited.
Printed in Great Britain.

High Street, c. 1910. The building on the right housing Hilton's Booterie had been a public
house called The Top Bull in the period 1855 to 1908. In the centre is Cheadle's market cross,
erected in the mid-seventeenth century and to the left of it stands PC Hillridge, on police duty
in the middle of the road. Of the three shops on the left of the road, the centre one housed the
Armed Services Recruitment Office during the First World War and was later to become the
Midland Bank and then Barclays Bank.

Contents

Introduction   7

1.   Schools and Churches   9

2.   Transport   23

3.   Societies and Social Occasions   39

4.   Around the Villages   67

5.   People at Work   101

6.   Cheadle Scenes   111

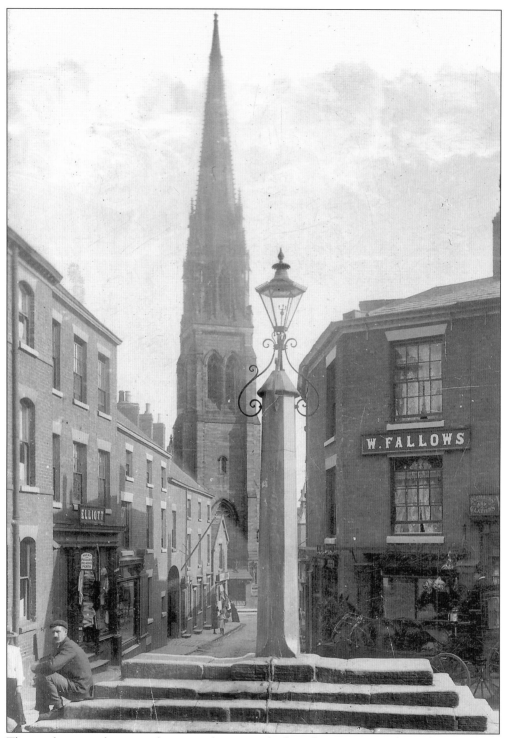

The market cross being used as a gas lamp standard in the 1900s. On the right is Fallows'
butchers shop, which was in business from 1834 until the 1920s. Looking down Cross Street can
be seen St Giles Roman Catholic church, which was built in 1846.

Introduction

In this, a second selection of photographs of Cheadle and the surrounding villages in this series, I have retained a similar format to one used in my previous book and tried to provide as much variety of subject material in the photographs themselves. I have again given equal prominence to people and buildings to represent the history of the area. I have included some photographs taken in the second half of the century in the hope that there will be many local people who will find someone they know in these pages.

I start the book by taking another look at the local churches and schools, which took a more central role in the life of the community in the earlier part of this century than they do now. I have included a chapter concentrating on transport. The twentieth century has seen both the rise and fall of railways in Cheadle and the only public transport system remaining today, in the form of buses, has a very limited scope now compared to the services provided by the variety of companies that used to ply their trade in the area.

A following chapter looks at social gatherings and occasions and these photographs reflect the importance of community in the lives of the people over the years. Indeed, this sense of belonging was often extended to the work place, which can be seen in some of the photographs in the chapter dealing with people at work.

The remaining chapters take us on a journey around the villages in the area and through Cheadle itself so that we can see what has changed and, also, what has remained the same.

In bringing this selection to you, I must thank all those who have loaned photographs from their private collections and family albums, so that their personal memories can gain a wider audience.

I hope that, in a world that is increasingly concentrating on the dawn of the next millennium, this book will provide further insight into life as it used to be in this area over the last hundred years or so of the current one.

W. George Short
Cheadle
June 1999

The Market Cross, Cheadle, looking west along High Street, *c.* 1910. Note the hardcore road.

A classic postcard from the *Views of Cheadle* series, published by Bernard Lowndes in the 1930s. Many of the photographs in this book were taken by him over a period of many years.

One
Schools and Churches

A gathering of parishioners outside the gates of St Giles parish church in the early 1920s. The building on the left was the National Boy's School at the time, but this closed in 1931 and the building then became the Carlos Institute. It was demolished in 1982 and the Cheadle rectory now stands on the site.

A wintry scene in the late 1930s showing The Terrace Steps which led directly onto the road. The churchyard gates and railings seen in this photograph were taken down during the Second World War and the metal was used for munitions.

Miss Agnes Watt in 1880. Miss Watt and a companion went on a holiday to Italy where she met Captain Lager, an officer in the Italian army. A friendship commenced and in due course Miss Watt and her companion returned to Cheadle. Captain Lager, who spoke very little English, came to England the following year and on arriving in London he asked for directions for 'Stok'. He was put on a train and when he arrived in Stoke he asked, in Italian, for a Miss Watt, the rector's daughter. The North Staffordshire Railway officials directed him to Blythe Bridge and then on to Cheadle by carriage (as Cheadle was not served by the railway at that time) and he duly arrived on the rectory doorstep. The friendship was re-kindled and he and Miss Watt were married by Revd Robert Watt, the Rector of Cheadle.

Cheadle Wesleyan Sunday school teachers in the 1940s. Back row, left to right: Dorothy Hall, Nora Hawley, Edna Wetwood, Reginald Williams, Hilda Beardmore and Edna Plant. Middle row: Mr Yarwood, Cyril Williams, Amy Mosley, Marion Hurst, Doris Alcock, Hilda Ratcliff, Edith Spragg, Florence Kinder, George Kinder and Hugh Shaw. Front row: Mr Forrester, Amy Shaw, Revd F.W. Henshall, Mr and Mrs W. Ratcliff, James Keates, Bagot Ball, Mrs Wood.

The Cheadle Choral Society, with guest singers from Wolverhampton, giving a concert in St Giles parish church in 1943. Blackout curtains cover the windows.

The weather vane taken down from the top of the steeple of the Cheadle Roman Catholic church for renovation in 1951. Seen here with the workmen is Father J. MacDonald, the parish priest from 1934 to 1956.

The Cheadle parish church Sunday school festival and procession being led to the church by the churchwardens, Mr W. Burton and Mr E.H. Lucas in the 1950s.

Cheadle church Mothers' Union on a visit to the Wedgwood factory at Barlaston in 1954. Back row, left to right: Mrs Walker, Mary Plant, Mrs Plant, Mrs Warren, Mrs Critchlow, Mrs Kinder, Mrs James, Mrs Wheat, -?-. Middle row: Mrs Williams, Mrs Bennett, Mrs Allen, Mrs Robinson, Mrs Jones (the rector's wife), Mrs Thorley, Mrs Burnett, Mrs Mycock, Mrs Allen, Mrs Bott and Mrs Burston. Front row: Mrs Booth, Mrs Lovatt, Mrs Turner, Miss Shenton, Mrs Charles, a lady from Freehay Mothers' Union, Mrs Malbon, Mrs Large and Mrs Slack.

The cast of the nativity play presented by members of the St Giles parish church in December 1957. The play was produced by the curate, Revd J.P. Ashton.

St Giles parish church garden party, held on the rectory lawns in June 1962. A selection of music was performed by members of the Cheadle Youth Orchestra, conducted by Mr K.C. Lovatt, during the afternoon.

Preb. S.E. Moore at his farewell service at St Giles parish church, attended by the five curates that he had trained during his ministry at Cheadle from February 1956 to May 1971. Left to right: Revd Malcolm Griffin (1959 to 1961), Revd Derek Smith (1966 to 1970), Revd David J.H. Jones (1970 to September 1972, when he resigned the ministry), Preb. S.E. Moore, Revd John Tomlinson (1962 to 1966) and Revd J.P. Ashton (1955 to 1959).

The Salvation Army Citadel in Ashbourne Road, Cheadle, which was built by J. Hurst Builders of Cheadle in 1935. This building is now owned by the Pentecostal Christian Fellowship Church.

The opening of the Salvation Army Citadel, Ashbourne Road, in December 1935. Back row, left to right: -?-, Mr W. Podmore (Chairman of Cheadle Rural District Council), Revd F.W. Henshall (Wesleyan), Mr J. Hurst (the builder) and Mr F.S. Cox (Clerk to Cheadle Rural District Council). Middle row: Mrs Helen Bird, Miss Barrett and Mrs Annie Shenton. Front row: -?-, Mr Harold Shenton, -?-, -?-, Revd Hon. Weld Forrester (Rector) and Revd F. Davis (Methodist from Froghall).

Interior of the Primitive Methodist chapel in Charles Street in September 1960. The chapel closed in 1964 and is now known as the Cecil Wedgwood Room.

Pupils of the Cheadle Junior School, Tean Road in 1918. Back row, left to right: Anne Chandler, Louisa Tongue and Elsie Alcock. Middle row: Emma Nutt, Ethel Locker, Jesse Thorley and Annie Campbell. Front row: Eve Clewlow, Jessie Hatton, Emma Wood, Nellie Moss and Edith Hurst.

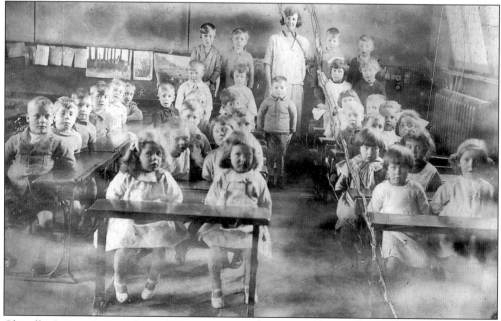

Cheadle County Primary School, Tean Road in 1927. Front row, left desk: Margaret and Betty Fox, right desk: -?- and Gwen Oakden. Second row, left desk: Ethel Reeves and Eunice Rhodes, right desk: Winnie Plant and -?-. Seated at the back is Fred Finney and standing at the back are George Thorley, Stanley Edwards and Prince Emery with the teacher, Miss Keates.

Cheadle Primary School concert held in the Wesleyan School Room in 1933. Back row, left to right: Nora Hawley, Nora Wright, Eileen Northwood, Eileen Barnes and Mary Whitehurst. Front row: Phylis Carnwell, Hilda Shaw, Doreen Alcock, Paul Dobson, Lorna Hurst, -?-, Betty Shaw and Marion Bloor. The girls' costumes were made of crepe paper.

Cheadle Church Junior Mixed School on 1 September 1951. Staff and periods of service: Back row: Mr B. Tootell (1947-55), Mrs M. Burch (nee Perrins,1940-52), Mrs M. Hurst (nee Burnett, 1950-73), Mrs E. Hutchins (nee Starkie, 1945-55), Mr J.E. Lees (1948-52). Front row: Miss P. Callant (1945-52), Miss A.J. Goodall (1924-60), Miss N.A. Marsh (headmistress, 1936-51), Miss M.J. Turner (1915-55), Mrs E.M. Stevenson (1948-55).

The choir and percussion group which performed at the dedication and official opening of the new extensions at the Bishop Rawle C. of E. (A) school on Thursday 16 June 1966. The opening ceremony was performed by the Rt Revd R.J. Clitheroe MA, Lord Bishop of Stafford. The new extensions comprised a fully equipped combined hall and gymnasium and a modern school kitchen.

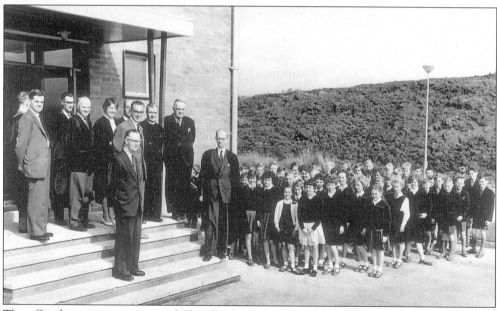

The official opening ceremony of Cheadle Grammar School on Wednesday 30 October 1963. Back row, left to right: Mr B.E.S. Trueman MA (teacher), Mr M.J.C. Read BSc, Mrs Searle BSc (nee Lamb), Mr T. Willis (county councillor). Middle row: Mr H. Stephenson (Assistant Education Officer), Mr F.D. Hughes BA (teacher), Mr R. Comley, Fr J. Connelly, Mr R.L. Carr (chairman of governors). Front row: Mr J.C. Cope (vice chairman) and Mr R.S. Baker MA BSc FRSA (headmaster 1962 to 1975). The Grammar school opened for the admission of students in September 1962 and closed on 31 July 1975. The school is now the Moorlands Sixth Form Centre.

School leavers outside the old school house at the Church School in 1927. Miss Ida Shufflebotham was the teacher and Mrs Fanny H. Coxon was the headmistress.

Staff and pupils from MacKenzie Secondary School setting off for a week's educational holiday in Paris in 1963. First left is Mrs Doreen Loane (teacher) and far right is Mr F.J. Gibbs (headmaster).

Cheadle Wesleyan Sunday school anniversary on 27 May 1928. On the left is Mr W. Ratcliff, the Sunday school superintendent and on the right is his daughter, Miss Ethel Ratcliff.

Two

Transport

A wagonette taking parishioners from Oakamoor Methodist church to the Woodhead Hall Sunday School anniversary celebrations in September 1910. Seated first and second on the left are Mr and Mrs Mellor and standing on the right are Mr and Mrs F. Holmes.

Sarah Matilda Tongue, who was born at the Ship Inn at Tenford, photographed on her bicycle around 1900. The small thatched building at the rear of the photograph was an outside toilet.

Edwardian 'cars' lined up at Moor Court prior to the start of a race held at Cotton around 1905.

Drivers taking a rest with their loaded wagons at Froghall Bridge on their way to Kingsley.

Some of the competitors in the Cotton race, *c.* 1905.

Mr James Lymer's wedding carriages outside Mr Lymer's home, No. 5, Stallington Road, Blythe Bridge, c. 1910. The driver on the left is Mr Williams and the driver on the right is Mr Lymer.

Dr Gibson and his wife in their car, registration number E 702, with Mr Thorley and their daughter Mary in May 1904. In the other car are Dr Gibson's assistant and their other daughter Elizabeth. They are inspecting the site of the Cheadle Isolation Hospital, Rakeway. The hospital; was on the site of what is now Beech Lodge Nursing Home.

Mr George Lymer and his 1908/9 Model 'T' Ford, which was used as a taxi in the area.

A photograph taken by Archie Holmes of a tyre change just outside Lichfield on a journey to the 1923 Wembley Exhibition. Standing on the left are John Hood, Ralph Keates and Fred Holmes. Frank Holmes is in front of the car, Wm Ball (Snr) is holding the tyre and Norman Keates is sitting in the car.

An 'Old Bill' Leyland bus standing at the Butlers Hill bus stop, *c.* 1924. Note the solid tyres.

Mr Joe Stephenson and Mr Prince Emery, driver and conductor with the Old Bill Bus Company. On 15 October 1932 the company was taken over by the Potteries Electric Traction Company Limited, which changed its name in the following year to Potteries Motor Traction Co. Ltd (PMT). Both Mr Stephenson and Mr Emery were employed by PMT, Mr Stephenson going on to become an inspector.

Mr James Lymer's second bus, a Guy Motor, registration EH 6436. The photograph, taken in 1926, shows his grandson, Aubrey Lymer, starting up the engine.

Mr Antony Mosley, maintenance fitter and driver for Shufflebotham and Tippers garage in High Street and the White Line Bus and Taxi Service from 1929 to 1932.

Cheadle Railway Company Limited built this station at Cheadle in 1900. Locomotion services were provided by the North Staffs Railway including the Manning Wardle engine shown here with a North Staffs Railway carriage (note the Stafford Knot crest). The North Staffs Railway took over the Cheadle Railway Company on 1 January 1908 and in 1909 they constructed an enlarged station and a house for the stationmaster.

New Haden Colliery at Brookhouses. Below the white house on the left is the entrance to the railway tunnel.

The railway sidings at the New Haden Colliery, Brookhouses.

Relatives and friends awaiting the departure of the train taking Cheadle enlisted men to Lichfield for army training in August 1914.

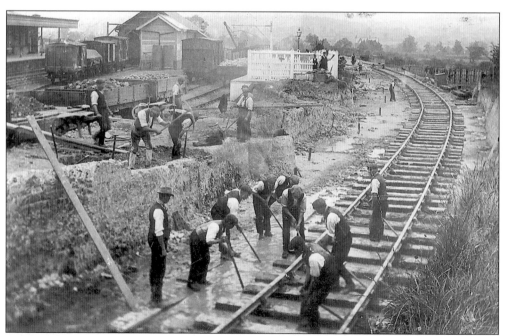

Extending the rail tracks and building loading bays at Cheadle Station in the late 1950s. These were necessary for the loading of gravel and aggregates from local quarries onto the trains.

This notice appeared on the Cheadle station notice board in February 1978.

British Railways Board
London Midland Region

Withdrawal of Public Freight Facilities

CHEADLE (Staffs)

The British Railways Board regret that it has been found necessary to withdraw public facilities for freight traffic at Cheadle (Staffs) with effect from Monday 6 March 1978.

Alternative facilities for freight traffic are available at Longport.

≷ British Rail

The last freight train on the Cheadle branch line, watched by pupils of the nearby Painsley School at 3pm on 16 November 1984. The driver was Mr R. Bromley, his assistant was Mr K. Lindop and the guard was Mr D. Watts.

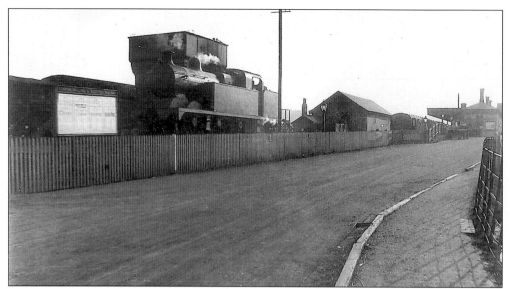

Cheadle station in the late 1950s showing a steam train taking on water from the water tower, which was demolished in July 1975. Note the timetable boards in the foreground.

Reg Smith's garage and showroom at Kingsley Moor in the 1970's, displaying cars for sale, from left to right: Austin A55 Mark II, Wolsley 1660, Morris Oxford, Austin A35 Van, Austin Mini, Morris Minor 1000, Austin A40 and Austin A60. The garage closed in 1987.

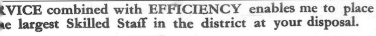

1935 SEPTEMBER 1935

SUN	MON	TUE	WED	THU	FRI	SAT
1	2	3	4	5	6	7
8	9	10	11	12	13	14
15	16	17	18	19	20	21
22	23	24	25	26	27	28
29	30	-	-	-	-	-

Reg Smith's garage in 1935. This calendar card, with a blotting pad on the reverse side, was a gift to customers.

Another calendar card for Reg Smith's garage showing his breakdown lorry.

In 1936 Mr Wm Plant Snr purchased two new Bedford lorries, registration numbers DEH 60 and DEH 61. The lorries were used to transport pottery and sanitary ware from the Potteries and bring back loads of milk and cheese from London and the South to United Dairies. They were later used to carry bricks from New Haden to the Swynnerton Ordnance Factory, loading and unloading by hand. The photograph shows Wm Plant Snr with his sons Fred and William Jnr at the rear of The White Hart in Tean, where the lorries were based.

Mr Bill Campbell, one of the last coal delivery merchants in the area when he retired in 1990. He is seen with his Ford lorry which cost £1,400 when purchased new in May 1968. When he started making deliveries in 1940, at the age of fourteen, there were no less than fourteen coal delivery men in Cheadle.

Hartley Bros, suppliers of mineral water, based in Kingsley. They made deliveries in the area in the 1950s.

Programme of events for the Cheadle Volunteer Fire Brigade demonstration in September 1895, at which the Cheadle Brigade won the competition. The brigade was taken over by the Cheadle RDC Fire Service in 1901.

The staff of Cheadle fire station in May 1956. Back row, left to right: Dennis Alkins, Walter Plant, Alf Wood, David Steele, Vin Pepper, Frank Dulson, Ernest Durose, Fred Spragg, Bert Snow, Ken Steele and Alan Bracking. Front row: Dennis Spencer, Ernie Hughes, Maurice Wilson, Sam Walker, Reg Mellor and Harold Nutt. The two engines on display are, on the left, a 1939 Leyland Pump Escape Engine named *Eveline*, registration number JRE 294 (this engine is still owned by the Staffordshire Fire Service) and, on the right, a Thornycroft 'Nubian' fire engine, registration 784 GRE.

Three
Societies and
Social Occasions

The Shaw family in 1890. Back row, left to right: Hugh (married Lizzie James), Lucy (died young), William (married, first, Winnie Campbell, second, Emmy Johnson), Alice (married Alex Marshall), Marie (married Jack Spooner), Sam (married Alice Green) and Lydia (married Alec Hurst). Front row: Bramwell (married Amy Campbell), Annie (married Sam Whitehurst), Samuel (the father), Grace (the youngest, married Ralph Kinder), Annie (the mother), Charles (married Ada Helena Wigley) and Norman (married Amy Plant).

Cheadle Town Football Club, around 1900. The players were, back row, left to right: G. Finney, T. Sutton, W. Roritson. Middle row: E. Plant, N. Goodby, W. Tipper. Front row: F. Johnson, I. Wood, F. Pirkin, A. Warrington, I. Austin.

Oakamoor Photographic Society 1908-10. Boys standing at the rear, from left to right: Albert Wilson, George Child, Richard Wilson. Seated: Dick Wilson, Mr Mellor, Mr Swinson (umpire of the cricket club), Elijah Jackson, Arthur Swinson, Jimmie Alcock, Sam Harvey and Enoch Berrisford.

A photograph of the Cheadle Board of Guardians of the Poor taken outside the old Cheadle Infirmary in 1915. The gentleman in the centre of the front row, with the white beard, is Mr Stephen Mear (chairman). Mr J.C. Keates and Mr J.R.B. Masefield, the representatives for Cheadle on the Board, are the fifth and sixth from the right on the centre row.

The Cheadle National Boys and Girls Infant School taking part in the Peace Celebrations Parade through the streets of Cheadle 19 July 1919.

Cheadle Juniors Football Club in 1920. The team, which played on the Recreation Ground, Tean Road, won three cups that year, The Sentinel Cup, The Longton Cup and one other. The photograph, which was taken at the rear of The Rising Sun public house, shows the cups and the replicas presented to the players. Back row, left to right: Mr Goldstraw, Mr Clewlow, Aubrey Finney, Bill Harris, Elijah Brunt, Mr Spooner, Mr Brunt and Mr Wright. Middle row: Lance Harris, Ernest Clarke, James Brunt, Harold Bentley, Reginald Kinder and Arthur Salt. Front row: Mr Wetwood, Bill Shaw, Sydney Bentley, Timmy Dale, Jack Davenport and Freddie Brunt.

Members of the Sir Wm Plant, Cheadle Lodge of the Royal Antediluvian Order of Buffaloes (which received its seal on 21 June 1921), assembled outside the gates of the Recreation Ground, Tean Road, after attending an Armistice church parade on 11 November 1923.

Oakamoor cricket ground in 1923. Oakamoor Cricket Club was the champion of the Cheadle and District School Cricket League in that year. Mr Primrose Thorley is pictured at the top of the steps.

The 1st Oakamoor Scout troop in 1923. Back row, left to right: B. Cope, M. Bowen, J. Murray, Jack Swinson, T. Bradbury, R. Mycock, C. Cartlidge and C. Goodwin. Middle row: S. Alkins, H. Shipley, C. Nichols, J. Dawson, Mr and Mrs Bearblock, H. Lucas, B. Salt, G. Tipper and E. Swinson. Front row: P. Bearblock, A. Charlesworth, B. Tipper and G. Lovell.

Cheadle Carnival fancy dress parade through High Street in 1927.

George Ernest Rushton, born in 1912 was one of eight children and suffered from infantile paralysis (Poliomyelitis). He never went to school but despite this he trained as an upholsterer at the Gobowen Cripples College in Shropshire. While there he designed and built a bicycle for himself on which the crank wheel and chain were placed on the top bar of the cycle frame. Instead of a pedal it was fitted with a leather handgrip which enabled the rider to propel the machine. George, pictured here with his bicycle in 1928, was presented to Prince George while at the college, to whom he demonstrated his riding skill.

One of T.R. Bailey's lorries being used in a 1930s carnival in High Street. The Royal Oak Hotel can be seen at the rear on the right of the picture.

The Green Valley Dance Band, Oakamoor in 1930. Back row, left to right: Albert Wilson, Frank Wooliscroft, Bert Brough, Albert Collier and Sydney Alkins. Front row: (a professional musician, Bert Beardmore, Kenneth Beardmore, Sam Walker, Peter Bearblock, Walter Forrester and Fred Bryan. Peterkin Bearblock produced this photograph as a Christmas card.

The re-opening of the Oakamoor Bowling Green on Easter Saturday, April 1930. Standing, left to right: Joseph Barker (collier), Will Leake, Fred Barker (stationmaster), Joseph Wooliscroft, Jack Heath, Tom Mellor, George Harrison, Will Alkins, Jack Alkins, Tom Wilson, Sam Walker, George Chadwick and Mr Wannah. Seated: Jack Wilson, Ernest Moseley, Michael Bolton and Tom Scott.

A group of Cheadle gentlemen at the old Cheadle cricket pavilion in 1933. Left to right: Mr Holbrook (workhouse master), Mr Birks (senior school headmaster), Dr E. Mackenzie (seated), Mr J.C. Keates (estate agent and representative of the Leek United Building society) and Mr Primrose Thorley (manager of the Froghall Ironstone Works).

Cheadle Carnival in 1937. The J. & N. Philips carnival float, using one of Wm Plant's lorries, under the name 'Dorcas Ladies'.

The J. & N. Philips of Tean Carnival Queen, Joyce Heath, with her attendants: Joan Wilson, Nellie Rowe, Daisy Beswick, Jessie Dale, Margaret Snow and Nancy Martin, and younger attendants Joan Slater and Jean Mosley holding her train, in 1937. This was the only occasion that the J. & N. Philips Tape Mill at Tean sponsored a Carnival Queen and she attended the Cheadle Carnival on the Greyhound Field. The girls were picked from different departments in the mill and the dresses were made in the sewing room.

Evelyn White, the 1939 Cheadle Carnival Queen. Evelyn was also appointed Hospital Queen for the North Staffs Royal Infirmary in August 1939.

The Cheadle Carnival Queen, sponsored by Brough Nicholson & Hall (owners of the 'Silk Mill'), in 1952. The company provided the dresses of platted silk ribbon and accessories. They also had a dray decorated for the occasion. Left to right: Mary Bridgett, Brenda Hall, Ruth Allen, Joseph Malkin, Margaret Gimbert (Carnival Queen), Madeline Smith, Sheila Byatt, Margaret Thorley, Megan Bates and Ivy Smith.

The 3rd Cheadle Guides and Brownies, formed by Revd A.E. Gibbons (Methodist minister) in 1941, with Marion James (Brown Owl) and Nora Hawley (Tawny Owl) sitting in the centre of the front row.

Camping at The Ranger, Dimmingsdale, in 1942. Standing, left to right: Alan Bradley, Ken Bradley, Alan Durose, Don Wardle and George Moss (Assistant Scout Leader). Seated: Gordon Rhodes, Garth Venables, Malcolm Boardman, Gerald Beardmore, Sam Forrester, Maurice Fletcher, Harold Hurst, Cecil Dickinson, Ken Plant, Peter Turner, Lance Northwood, Bill Mosley and Sidney Spooner.

The 2nd Cheadle Rover Scouts, hiking on the Weaver Hills in 1942. Standing, left to right: Ken Bradley, Alan Durose, Harold Hurst, Eric Whitehurst, Philip Egerton and Derek Plant. Seated: Donald Wardle, Bert Emery, Sidney Spooner and Eric Palmer. Donald Wardle received his King's Scout Badge from the Chief Scout, Lord Rowallan, 12 July 1947.

Enrolment of the 2nd Cheadle Rover Scouts at Cheadle Parish Church in 1942. Back row, left to right: Philip Egerton, Peter Turner, Don McKinnon, Alan Durose, George Moss and Harold Hurst. Front row: Eric Palmer (wearing the white shirt and beret of the Air Scouts), Sidney Spooner, Revd Oswald Ede, Mr Del-Strother (Scout Commissioner), Cecil Dickinson, Donald Wardle, Ron Slack and Gordon Rhodes.

Cheadle Town Band, shown in Queen Street. The band played around the town on Christmas mornings until the 1940s.

Members of the Cresswell Home Guard in October 1940 leaving their training ground, the cricket ground at the top of the photograph on the right, and passing the Isaac Walton Inn, led by Sergeant Shaw, a member from Draycott.

The Carlos Players in a production of *The Man from the Ministry* in 1950. Back row, left to right: Bill Potts, Bert Keates, A.B. Hurst, Miss Collier, Revd H. Barton, Mrs N. Chell, Mrs Brown and Mr K. Chell. Front row, seated: Mr W. Brown, Mr A. Collier, Miss M. Keates and Mr H. Wardle.

Royal British Legion (Women's Section) Sale of work on 3 December 1949. Standing, left to right: Mrs W. Raine, Mrs Elliott, Mrs Berry, -?-, Mrs Chell. Seated: Miss W. Underhill, Mrs Barton Land, Miss A. Barker, Mrs C. Collis, Mrs Parr, Mr Lamont.

Officials of the Cheadle and District Festival of Britain Celebrations held on the Cheadle Cricket Field on Saturday 8 August 1951. Left to right: Mr F.J. Gibbs (headmaster), Flt Lt D. McWhirter (RAF Cheadle), Mr P. Harrison (Cheadle Parish councillor), Dr E.H. Evison (president), Mr B. Snow (chairman), Mrs R. Berry (Cheadle Parish councillor), Mr S.J. Looker (county councillor) and Mr R.J. Wardle (festival organiser).

An afternoon of leisure at No. 1 bowling green at Cheadle Recreation Ground. The onlookers were, standing: Clem Whitehurst and, seated: Jessie Whitehurst, Billy Cotton, Joe Brunt and George Lowell. The players were: Harold Lovatt, Aubrey Lovatt, Arthur Plant and Tom Alcock.

Pigeon fanciers, Bert Whitehurst, Arthur Bailey and Lance Harris, awaiting the return of their birds at the Mill Road Lofts in 1980.

The New Melody Stars Band, photographed at The Crown Hotel, Stone, in the 1960s. Left to right: Derek Burton, Arthur Parker, George Dawson, Bill Mason, George Kent and Alan Ainsworth.

The MacKenzie School Orchestra, formed in 1955 by Mr K.C. Lovatt, head of the music department. Standing, left to right: Hugh Lovatt, Alan Spooner and John Seabridge. Seated: Graham Smith, Cameron Howes, George Smith, Michael Wilson, Jim Plant, Malcolm Plant and John Carr. The pianist was Norbert Collier.

Cheadle Youth Orchestra on the stage of the MacKenzie school hall in 1966. The orchestra was formed as the Mackenzie School Orchestra in 1955 with eleven players (see previous photograph) and when the founder, Mr K.C. Lovatt, retired in 1992 the orchestra had seventy five players. In 1986, the orchestra played at the opening of the National Garden Festival in Stoke on Trent, in the presence of HM The Queen. They have recorded programmes for Radio Stoke and, over the years, they have raised thousands of pounds for local charities.

The first annual dinner of the Cheadle Swimming Baths Supporters Club, held at the Guild Hall on 17 November 1960. Standing, left to right: Mr Colclough, Mr Salt, Mr J. Spooner, Mr Porter, Mrs Godwin, Mrs Carr, Mrs Porter, Mr Lovatt, Mr Godwin, Mr and Mrs Swinson, Mr Carr, Mr and Mrs Kent, Mr and Mrs K. Chell, with Mr A. Moult in the background. Seated: Mrs Colclough, Mr and Mrs T. Willis, Mr and Mrs G. Maddicot and Mr Campbell. The above committee, along with their supporters, raised the money to build the Cheadle Swimming Baths which were opened on 2 September 1967.

Thomas Bolton of Froghall Hockey Team in October 1964. Back row, left to right: John Walker, Mike Rogers, Arthur Gilbert, Ted Small, Herbert Capewell, Peter Wilson and K. Mascurine. Front row: Barry Williams, Robin Wood, Chris Elks, Mick Pointon and Alan Thorley.

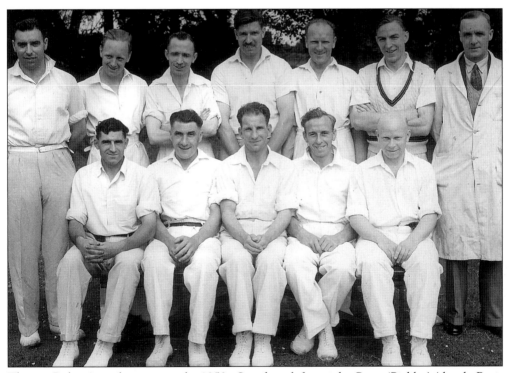

Thomas Bolton's cricket team in the 1950s. Standing, left to right: Percy 'Pickles' Alcock, Boris Alcock, Stan Capewell, Herbert Capewell, Norman Heathcote, Arthur Gilbert and an umpire from the league. Seated: Bill 'Crash' Rushton, Jimmie Brunt, Bert Whitehurst, Jack Sales and Lance Harris.

Tean Tennis Club, which played on the tennis courts at Oakhill, Tean, in 1938. Back row, left to right: Bill Edwards, Peter Parkinson, Philip Fazackerly, Mr Munday and three workers from J. & N. Philips' Manchester works. Front row: -?-, Beattie Tipper, Miss Garner, -?-, May Spooner, -?-, Elsie Jones, Nancy Slater, Dorothy Munday.

J. & N. Philips' Tean hockey team photographed behind Tenford Mill in the 1930s. Back row, left to right: Audrey Boon, Phyllis Rowe, Marie Spooner, -?-, Kath Mellor, Margaret Snow. Front row: Eddie Moss, May Spooner, Nora Rushton, Nora Oakden (the goalkeeper), Dorothy Inskip.

J. & N. Philips' Tean sports team in the inter company sports match versus Manchester, outside Tean Hall in 1938. Back row, left to right: Nora Oakden, May Spooner, Bill Edwards, Miss Garner, Mr Mills, Miss Spearing and Marie Spooner. Front row: Dorothy Inskip, Barbara Allen, Joyce Spooner, -?-, Mr Percy Stephens, May Grocott, -?-, Miss Bolton, Nora Rushton.

J. & N. Philips' Tean sports team again in the inter company sports match versus Manchester, outside Tean Hall in 1938. From left to right: Joyce Brindley, Nancy Prime, Gwen Oakden, Blance Moss, Nora Oakden, May Spooner.

The Cheadle Choral Society's production of *The Gondoliers* at the Carlos Institute in 1953. The principals, pictured here, were Margaret Lovatt, behind Len Keates, Arthur Gilbert and Marjorie Moss. The orchestra was conducted by Mr John Fenna.

The Cheadle Choral Society production for 1955 was *Yeoman of the Guard*. Front row, left to right: Bill Forrester, Dorothy Fowell, Peter Wright, Ena Ratcliffe, Ron Evernden, Margaret Lovatt, Len Keates, Arthur Gilbert, Kath Keates, Mary Ladkin, Maureen Wood and Bert Emery.

In 1964, the production chosen by the Society was *Iolanthe*. From left to right: Gordon Alcock, Eric Shaw, Margaret Morrison, Peter Wright, Norbert Collier and Arthur Gilbert.

HMS Pinafore was performed by the Cheadle Choral Society in 1965. Arthur Gilbert as Sir Joseph Porter, Gordon Alcock as Captain Coran and David Gilbert as Midshipman.

Cheadle Choral Society's *Showboat* float. Back row, left to right: Michael Lovatt, Dennis Vickers, Roy Hedges, Eric Plant, Les Gilbert, Fred Spragg and Arthur Gilbert. Middle row: Wilf Bentley, Wendy Gilbert, Edna Kinder, Jean Bentley, Margaret Scragg, Brenda Shenton, Jenny Chapman and Christine Withers. Front row: Hilary Edwards, Sheila Lovatt, Miriam Birch, Rosalynd Birch, Sarah Lovatt, Margaret Beardmore, Eyvone Saint, Mary Ladkin and Lance Harris.

Creating the float for the Cheadle Choral Society entry for the Cheadle Festival in 1977 on the council car park in Harbourne Road.

The Tean Young Wives Group was founded in March 1968 by Mrs Janet Willson, wife of the Methodist Minister for Tean, Revd M. Willson. This photograph was taken at Mrs Willson's farewell party held at the Methodist Sunday school room, Gorsty Hill, Tean in August 1970. Left to right: Mrs Margaret Tickle, Mrs Christine Harrop, Mrs Teresa Saunders, Mrs Betty Hart, Mrs Joyce Plant, Mrs Janet Willson, Mrs Pam O'Hara, Mrs Sheila Blaize, Mrs Dorothy Mellor and Mrs Kath Brough. The Young Wives Group changed its name to the Tean Ladies Group in January 1973 and went on to provide popular fortnightly meetings and outings. However, times changed and the group closed at the end of 1984.

Gentleman's fancy dress cricket team at Bent House Farm in the 1960s. Back row, left to right: Graham Forrester, Ray Starkey, Ray Heath, Alec Shaw and Eli Brunt. Front row: Cyril Forrester, Reg Bentley, Pat McGarry, Chris Stone, Ted Eaton and Terry Plant.

Ladies' fancy dress cricket team at Bent House Farm in the 1960s. Back row, left to right: Margaret Plant, May Plant, Elsie Slater, Dolly Whitehurst, Betty Beaman, June Plant and Florence Groves. Front row: Betty Barker, Doris Wheat and Mary Shakeshaft.

Four
Around the Villages

St Mary's Roman Catholic church, Cresswell, which was built in 1816 by the Stourton family, who owned the Draycott estates, at a cost of £800. The presbytery, the white building at the rear of the church, was used as a seminary for the preparation of young men for the priesthood. Among the students was Francis Fairfax, the first priest at St Giles Roman Catholic church in Cheadle.

St Margaret's church, Draycott in the Moors, *c*. 1920. It was built and consecrated in 1268, but several alterations have been made since then. In 1931 the open space in the foreground started to be used as an extension of the churchyard.

The 'Old Cottages' in Cheadle Road, Draycott, *c*. 1910. The house on the left had the roof relaid with tiles in 1928 and sometime later the house on the right was demolished.

A view of the A50 road from Blythe Bridge to Uttoxeter as it passes through the rural setting of Draycott in the 1920s. Bungalows now stand on the site of the farm buildings on the left.

On Tuesday 3 January 1978 this consignment of wheels for the new British Rail train, en route for Derby, came adrift from a transporter vehicle as it rounded an uphill curve on the narrow A50 road at Draycott in the Moors.

'Oakhill' in Upper Tean, which was built in 1689 as a private residence. In the early nineteenth century it was occupied by Revd C.B. Charlewood, who laid the foundation stone of Christ Church, Upper Tean, on 20 June 1842. The house later became one of the family homes of the Philips family. During the Second World War it was used by the RAF, but it has since returned to private ownership.

Troops and equipment in Upper Tean, en route to the Lichfield Barracks during the First World War.

The fight for the Tean By-pass. On 2 November 1977, Rt Hon. Mr William Rodgers, Minister of Transport, visited Tean to listen to all points of view and conduct a personal investigation into conditions on the busy A50. Here we see Mr Rodgers listening to comments from a member of the Tean Valley Action Group with Mrs Joyce Plant, the group's press officer, holding the banner. Work started on the by-pass in January 1983 and was completed and opened on 3 April 1985, some forty seven years after Tean was first considered for a by-pass.

High Street, Tean showing The White Hart and The Black's Head, two of the eight public houses in Tean at this time, *c.* 1905.

The Providence chapel in New Road, Tean was built in 1822. It was linked with the Bethel chapel in Cheadle by Revd John Tallis and Revd John Bull, ministers of both chapels. The chapel and parishioners merged with the United Reform church in 1972 and they were united with the Methodist church in 1984. The chapel closed on 30 March 1987. The building is now privately owned.

Mr and Mrs Arthur Farmer outside their shop on the corner of Uttoxeter Road in Tean around 1935.

The Heybridge in Lower Tean, built in 1813 by the Philips family and occupied by successive members of the family until it was demolished in the 1950s.

Hollington Road, Tean in the days before tarmacadam roads.

St Mary and All Saints church, Checkley in 1916. It was consecrated in 1196 by Hugh de Nonant, the 42nd Bishop of Coventry and Lichfield. The patronage at that time was held by the Beke family. The church is a Grade 1 listed building.

St Mary and All Saints church, Checkley. Records show that in 1550 'Anthony Draycott put in coloured glass in the clerestory windows and oak stalls in the chancel'.

The chapel and stained glass windows in the south aisle of Checkley church were erected in 1922 to the design of J.N. Comper. They were donated by Mr and Mrs Morton Philips of The Heybridge, Lower Tean, in memory of their son, Mark, who was killed in the First World War.

High Street, Tean in the days of horse-drawn deliveries. On the left is The Black's Head public house. On the right, in the middle distance, is the three storey tape mill built by J. & N. Philips in 1822 and the nearer four storey mill built in 1885.

The Blacksmith's Arms public house at the east end of High Street, Tean. First recorded in 1872 it closed down in 1978.

A British Army tank being transported through Tean during the Second World War. The photograph was taken from outside the Methodist church which stood at the apex of New Road and Old Road. The church was demolished in 1987.

The Anchor Inn at Tenford. A public house has stood on this site for over 200 years.

The Huntley Toll Gate House, built in 1818 at a cost of £63. Within the quote were 'window cases of good oak with good glass over the top of the first floor, the beam to carry the weight in front to be of good oak 10in x 9in and at the side to be 8in x 7in'. The Toll Gate House was sold into private hands in 1878.

The front doorway of Huntley Hall with two members of the Mather family in residence.

Huntley Hall, built in the 1820s for Captain Clement Sneyd RN. On his death in 1851 the hall passed to his daughter and her family. In the sale of the Huntley Hall Estate in March 1927 the Hall was Lot 1 of a 15 lot sale. The Hall was described as 'a capital country residence' containing lounge, hall, dining room, smoke room and drawing room on the ground floor with domestic offices (kitchen, etc.) and eight bedrooms on the first floor and maid's accommodation on the second floor. Outside there was stabling and outbuildings and 15 acres of land. The centre part of the hall was demolished in 1929.

The Crown Inn at Mobberley at the turn of the century. The Crown Inn is first mentioned in the directories of Staffordshire in 1834, when William Travis was the licensee.

Cheadle Methodist church garden fete held at Plantation House in 1922. Plantation House was built by the Mackenzie family in 1855.

Winnoth Dale Methodist chapel, known locally as 'The Chapel in the Valley'. Opened in 1899, families remember the many happy occasions there and those that attended, amongst those Mrs Winnie Rushton who was the organist for many years. The chapel closed in 1969 and was remembered in a poem 'In a little chapel on Winnoth Dale Way, We used to worship and to pray'. It is now privately owned and used for storage purposes.

Harewood Park, Leek Road, Cheadle in 1906. It was built in the 1860s by Mr W.E. Bowers as a gentleman's residence.

Hales Hall pond on Oakamoor Road being drained to clear algae and refuse away in 1978. In some parts the depth of the pond is between 12 and 14 ft.

A wedding reception in 1909 at Lightoaks in Oakamoor, one of the family homes of the Bolton family.

Woodbank in Oakamoor, built in 1833. The directories of Staffordshire for 1834 state that Mr Joseph Ingleby, the 'master' at the brassworks at Oakamoor was resident. It was later purchased by the Bolton family.

THE BRIDGE, OAKAMOOR

Oakamoor bridge in the 1920s. The first recorded bridge was one of wooden construction which was replaced by one of stone in 1709. This bridge was widened in 1778 to meet turnpike requirements. The bridge is today maintained by Staffordshire County Council.

The road to Stoneydale in Oakamoor in the 1920s. The River Churnet runs below the wall to the left and the drive leading off to the right leads to The Lodge.

Oakamoor Lodge was built in 1761 by George Kendall, the manager of the Oakamoor mill. In the early 1800s the Wragge family moved in and at about 1875 it was sold to Mr Thomas Bolton. At the turn of this century one of his sisters, Sarah, married Dr Bearblock and they took up residence, remaining there until they died in 1948 and 1951 respectively. The Lodge was demolished soon afterwards.

Mr Robinson mowing at Banks Farm, Oakamoor in the 1920s. Note the farmhand on the right sharpening the blade.

The floods at Oakamoor in 1927, showing the residents of the houses at the island being helped out of their homes by boat. The structure on the left is the end of the works building.

Oakamoor railway station in the 1950s. The station was opened by the North Staffordshire Railway on 13 June 1849, closed to passenger traffic on 4 January 1965 and closed to goods traffic on 3 October 1965. The steam train in the photograph is coming from Alton and the branch lines going off to the left lead to the copper mill of Thomas Bolton & Sons.

The Cock Inn at Kingsley Holt. This public house closed in the 1980s and then reopened as the Lion and Hounds. It is now a private house. The building on the left was built in the 1920s as a bakery, later to be used as a garage for Mr Powell's charabanc which was used for services to Cheadle and for hire.

Froghall Toll Gate House. This closed as a Toll House in 1878. The road in the centre of the photograph leads to Whiston and the bridge in the foreground leads over the railway line and on to the Froghall limestone quarry sidings.

Froghall in the 1930s. On the right, in the foreground, is the Methodist chapel with the football ground to the left and the Cheadle Road leading off into the distance. Of the six cottages seen top right, the first from the left was a shop and number six was the post office. On the left hand side of the road is the Railway Inn.

The Navigation Inn, Froghall. An Ansells Brewery public house, the last licensee when it closed in 1958 was Mr Walter Sales.

Kingsley school, *c.* 1880. Back row, left to right: Rupert Alcock, Tom Forrester, Minnie Carr, Miss Sargeant, Mrs Pollock, Polly Carr, Mr Smith (schoolmaster), Simon Goodwin. Middle row: Polly Jackson, Annie Forrester, Minnie Sutton, Mr Pollock (rector), Annie Carr, Isobel Smith, Tommy Carr. Front row: Jonah Billings, Colin Smith, Joe Carr, Will Fenna, Tom Smith, William Adams, Charlie Forrester. Standing at the right was Billy Bradshaw, who was blind.

Kingsley in 1910. On the left is The Royal Oak public house, of which Mr Morton was the licensee at the time. On the right are the Buntings Brewery delivery carts and horses taking a break.

Outside The Swan public house in Kingsley High Street in 1906. On the left, with the white horse, is Mr George Buckett who was a farmer from Hazles Cross. On the right is Harry Poyser, a horse captain. On the corner, below The Swan, stood The Cosy Corner Picture Drome which was demolished in February 1966.

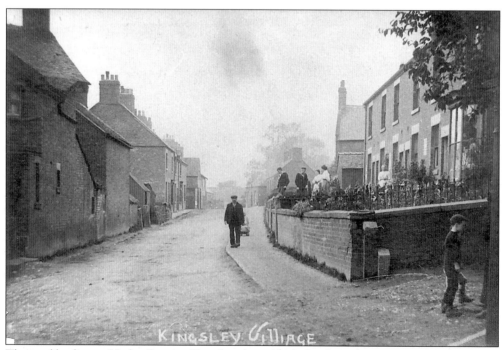

The road leading to Hazles Cross in Kingsley about 1910. On the right is a row of houses known as Shepherd's Row or Parliament Row, which were built in the mid 1800s by Miss Shepherd.

Kingsley Tithe Award dated 27 June 1839 lists this house as Award No. 331, owned by Kingsley church and occupied by Revd Robert Haynes. It was described as 'Rectory House, buildings with garden, area 1 rood and 17 perch'. In 1845 the new rectory was built and this house is now in private ownership.

St Wilfred's church, Cotton which was 'solemnly opened' on Easter Tuesday, 25 April 1848. Bishop Wiseman sang the mass and Father Newman preached. The architect was A.W.N. Pugin and the Earl of Shrewsbury gave £2,500 towards the cost of construction. To the left of the steeple is Cotton Hall, the deeds of which date back to 1601 in the family name of Gilbert. The hall was converted to a school in 1868.

Father Faber's Retreat, Cotton, a shrine dedicated to 'Our Lady of Lasalette'. Built by Father Faber in 1848, the shrine was repainted and refurbished in 1956 by one of the masters of the college. It was unfortunately vandalised some twenty years ago.

The refectory at Cotton College in the 1930s. Many of the students attended the college with a view to receiving instructions and guidance on becoming Roman Catholic priests.

The cloister at Cotton College. The Sedgeley Park Preparatory School took over the buildings in 1868 and extensions were added in 1874, 1886 and again in 1931. The school closed in July 1987.

Dedication of the Cotton Mothers' Union standard at St John the Baptist church, Cotton in the early 1950s. The banner is held by Mrs G. Lees with Mrs Edge and Mrs Billings as string bearers. In attendance are Revd Alfred Jones, the Rural Dean and Revd Hugh Rogers, vicar of Oakamoor and Cotton.

Cotton Mothers' Union sale of work at Vic Alcock's caravan park in 1984. The three gentlemen on the back row towards the left of the photograph are, from left to right: Vic Alcock, Revd H.B. Harrop and Revd W. Goldstraw.

The Star Inn at Cotton in the 1920s. The original inn was called The Blazing Star.

The Shrewsbury Arms public house, Alton, which was built in the late 1800s to replace the former Shrewsbury Arms which stood on the Farley Road. In May 1965 permission was granted for a change of name to The Wild Duck Inn.

The Temperance and Refreshment Room, Alton, in the 1920s. In the 1970s the then licensee applied for and was granted permission to change from temperance status to one where alcohol could be served.

King Edward VII passed through Alton on his way to Alton Towers on the morning of 21 November 1907. He had previously passed through Cheadle and after visiting the Towers he planted a tree and then proceeded on his tour of the area via Uttoxeter.

Denstone College Chapel in 1914. The chapel was dedicated by the Lord Bishop of Lichfield, Bishop Selwyn, on 27 July 1887.

Denstone College, showing the Lonsdale Quadrangle. The foundation stone of the college was laid on 22 October 1868 by Bishop Lonsdale and the construction of the school was finished in 1872. The building was dedicated on 29 July 1873 and it opened on 9 October 1873.

The Blacksmith's Arms, Foxt. This public house was de-licensed by Mr Israel Beard in the early 1900s but then became a corn store.

A local band leading a Peace Celebrations March past The Woodcutter's Arms and around the village of Foxt in 1919.

A group of parishioners sitting outside Foxt Church after the Peace Celebrations March in 1919.

Wootton Hall, which was built in 1730. For generations it was the home of the Bromley Davenport family. The hall was offered for sale in 1929 and again in 1930 and 1931, but no buyers could be found. The hall was eventually bought 'for the stone' by the county council for £8,000. The hall was demolished in 1931, some of the stone being used for the renovation of the hanging bridge at Mayfield and part of the facade stone being used to build a bungalow at Waterfall. The staircase was purchased by a local gentleman who had it built into his own hall.

Five
People at Work

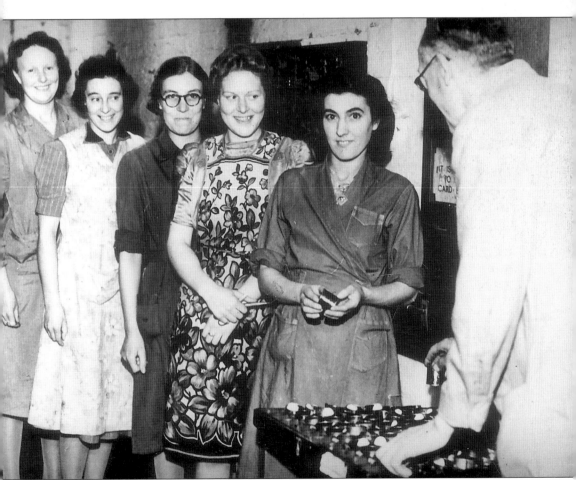

Mr Percy Stephens, in 1935, paying out the wages to the workers at J. & N. Philips' Tean Mill. Left to right: Nancy Slater, Joyce Heath, Evelyn Mount, Sylvia Allen and May Bull. The wages at this time were 15s per fortnight.

Mr and Mrs Pegg at the Cupola Mill Water Wheel. This mill closed down around 1900 because of the unreliable water supply.

The Cupola Mill. In the late 1700s it was used for grinding frit for Froghall and later lead ore was smelted there. The furnace was used for making bricks by Bothams Brick Works around 1900.

The finishing shop at J. & N. Philips' Tean Mill in 1928. Front row, left to right: Miss Nicklin, Nancy Holmes, Nellie Bentley. Second row: Nancy Bevans, -?-, Florence Beaman. The operatives in this department worked from 8am to 6pm, with meal breaks. When working overtime they stayed until 7pm. The wage, for a normal six day week was 8s 2d, paid fortnightly. If an extra hour was worked the wage was increased by 2d per day.

A Christmas party at the Brough Nicholson and Hall Silk Mill in Oakamoor Road, Cheadle, in the 1950s. Back row, left to right: Audrey Spooner, Marie Alcock, Mabel Lovatt, Phyllis Harvey, Muriel Hall, Joan Allen and Jean Woodward. Front row: Ethel Clark, Jean Fox, Nora Jackson, Phyllis Summerfield and Lily Harvey.

Staff in the new ribbon shed at the Brough Nicholson and Hall Silk Mill in 1934. Back row, left to right: Eddie Jones, Dolly Mullinor, Dora Robertson, Eunice Rhodes, Margaret Myatt, Lily Brunt, Eileen Snow, Mabel Lovatt and Jim Bates. Middle row: Henri Probst, Charlie Sleigh, Miss Carr, Beattie Salt, Mary Alcock, Katie Robins and Mrs Brunt. Front row: Sarah Hordern, Marie Clark, Henri Knech, Blance Robertson, Daisy Bates and Elsie Heath.

The five Walker brothers, seen here on the nine hole golf course at Longhurst Farm, Oakamoor, in 1910, had a total of 250 years of service with Thomas Bolton & Sons Limited. From left to right: Fred Walker (Froghall works manager), William Walker (Widnes works), T. Walker (Widnes works), S. Walker (Oakamoor and Froghall works) and John Walker (Oakamoor and Froghall works).

'Charcoal Jack', a charcoal burner by trade, around 1910. He is seen here laying the timbers to make a charcoal fire. It is said that he would never allow anyone to be in the vicinity while he was lighting a fire. The hut in the background was Jack's home while working on the site.

Mr Hanson Green and his men with the block and tackle that they used to load tree trunks on to the cart.

Employees of Wm Ball, builders of the Silk Mill for Brough Nicholson and Hall in 1899. Standing, left to right: Will Keates, Sid Waugh, Jack 'Codin' Summerfield, Ern Powell and Peter Emmett. Seated: John Lovatt, Jim Shakeshaft, Joe Nutt, Uriah Prince, Mr Beardmore and Jimmy Bridgett.

Tacklers, maintenance and managerial staff at the Silk Mill in 1935. Back row, left to right: Henri Knech, Reg Ward, Fred Spooner, Charles Sleigh, Henri Probst, Cyril Spooner, Arthur Spooner, John Lovatt, Bagot Ball, Bill Reid, Aubrey James and Wilfred Shaw (manager of the Cheadle Silk Mill). Middle row: Alf Malkin, Bernard Crook, Fred Plant, Jim Bates, Arthur Pyatt, Alf Hatton, Oswald Crook, Bill Lowndes and Steve Summerfield. Front row: Leslie Spooner, Fred Lovatt, Jackie Summerfield, Will Lowndes, Ken Crook and David Orr-Lovatt.

Employees who had completed forty years service with Brough Nicholson and Hall at the Silk Mill in Cheadle in 1955. Back row, left to right: Steve Summerfield, Will Lowndes, Harold Pegg (manager), John Lovatt and Mrs Louie Plant. Front row: Mrs Elsie Hatton, Mrs Sarah Beardmore, Mrs Annie Key and Mrs Emma Twigg.

The retirement of Mr Otto Hoehn, manager (centre, wearing spectacles) at the Brough Nicholson and Hall Silk Mill in the early 1950s.

Flood water in the Thomas Bolton's strip mill at Oakamoor in July 1927.

A train crash at the Thomas Bolton's works in Froghall in 1944.

The last train load of sand from the British Industrial Sand plant at Moneystone in August 1988.

The refinery at the Thomas Boltons works in Froghall. Mr Roland Beardmore, the tap hole attendant at the reverbatory furnace which was heated to 800 degrees centigrade to ensure that the metal remained liquid until after it reached the moulds.

110

Six
Cheadle Scenes

Clearing snow from the roof of The Beeches in the 1930s. The Beeches stood at the east end of the High Street and was demolished in 1961. This was the home of Dr G. Saint. On the left of the photograph is the lamp bracket of the post office.

The printing offices of the *Cheadle and Tean Times* until 1961. These premises were then demolished to make way for the new shopping area. When opened in 1962, the shops included Woolworths and Fine Fare.

Mr Roland Machin standing outside his printing office at 14 High Street in the 1920s. Mr Machin's father came to Cheadle in the 1870s and was responsible for publishing and printing Cheadle's first local newspaper, *The Cheadle Herald* on 8 September 1877.

The bakery and confectioners at 24 High Street belonging to Mr F. Abberley. Records state that Mr Abberley was trading there from 1904 to 1912.

The Unicorn Inn in High Street around 1900, with Jabez Noden and his family outside. Mr Noden was licensee from 1882 to 1916. The inn closed its doors for the last time on 9 April 1961 and the building was then demolished.

A 1910 view of the east end of High Street. Note the wide pavement and narrow road. On the left is Wooliscroft's grocery and off licence. Next to this are two private houses, in one of which Mrs Harvey, the local midwife, lived.

The north side of High Street showing 'Babyland' which opened on Wakes Saturday, September 1953. Next door was Mr Cliff, the butcher and then the furniture showroom of Mr W.R. Alcock, 1955 to 1960. Next to that was Mr J.E. Goodwin, baker and confectioner.

The south side of High Street in the early 1960's, showing W.R. Alcock's Stafford House showroom and then two private houses and The Greyhound Inn. This public house closed on 14 September 1962 and the building was converted into Barclays Bank.

Mr Arthur Emery, Mr George Lees and Mr Harold Lees in front of Lees butchers shop, 41 High Street, in 1929.

Looking west along Cheadle High Street, *c.* 1900. On the left is Heath's butchers, later Lees, and Ralph Keates tea rooms. On the right is Amies Boot and Shoe Store. Note the hardcore road and the meat on the table in front of the butcher's shop.

The centre of High Street in 1925. On the right is Marshall's chemist shop with the privet hedge, the pillars and the balcony. The shop entrance, as seen here, was at the side from the 1890s until the 1920s. The balcony over the doorway was used by Mr Jacob Lowndes and his son Bernard as a vantage point from which to take photographs of occasions and happenings in the Market Square opposite.

A gathering of people, including members of the Independent Order of Oddfellows, in the Market Square in 1910, with a band playing in the foreground.

Circus elephants processing along the High Street in the 1960s.

Looking up Cross Street at the turn of the century. W.J. Smith was a grocers shop up until 1908. Tipper & Sons were drapers in High Street from 1860 to 1936.

A bird's eye view of Cheadle from the parish church tower, before 1894 when an extension was built on to the school building in the foreground. On the left is Back Street, now Prince George Street. The chimney in the distance is that of the Tape Mill which was built in 1864.

The same view from the tower taken in 1996. The school in the foreground has been replaced by the new rectory. The major difference to be seen is the extension of the town into the distance by the building of new housing estates.

Tudor House in High Street. Built in 1558, this is now the oldest building in Cheadle. The facade seen in this photograph was removed in 1907 and the traditional woodwork of tudor buildings was discovered under the plaster. This was then treated and it has remained exposed since then. The building was occupied by Allards, saddlers and harness makers, from 1880 to 1940 and Mrs Moss, grocer and fruiterer, traded from the adjoining premises between 1900 and 1924.

The fountain, to the right of the photograph, was erected in 1879 as a gift to the town from the Bourne family. Cumberland House, the three storey building in the centre, was built in 1745. To the left are the steps leading up to the terrace.

The Terrace in 1910. The steps on the left of the photograph led up to the old parish church up until 1837. The telegraph pole shows that there were eight subscribers connected at the time, the first telephone in Cheadle being connected in 1904. Ambledon's music shop can be seen in the distance, of which Amos Smith was manager and agent.

A 1903 view of the parish church, with the spire of the Roman Catholic church seeming to rise out of the tower.

The demolition, in August 1982, of what had once been, between 1793 and 1908, the Jug and Glass public house. The building had subsequently been used as a private residence. On the right is the sign bracket of the Swan public house which also opened in 1793 and which closed in June 1998. It is to be refurbished and reopened in 1999.

Rose Hill, Town End, Cheadle. In 1814 John Blagg bought a converted farm cottage in Cheadle, then called Primrose Hill. He extended the property, laid out the grounds and renamed it Rose Hill. The family moved into it in 1815 and it remained in the Blagg and Masefield families until 1946.

The New Inn at Brookhouses. First mentioned in the Cheadle directories in 1834, it was renamed The Huntsman while Don Johnson was the licensee between 1953 and 1956.

Cheadle Infirmary was built in 1901 by J. Gallimore to the design of J. Snape at a total cost, including the laundry, of £9,749 19s 6d. It was demolished in 1987 to make way for the new Cheadle Hospital which opened on 26 June 1989.On the left of the photograph is part of the original three storey workhouse which was built in 1775.

The opening of the Cheadle Ex-Service Centre in Bank Street on 2 November 1946. The photograph shows Dr A.G. Coullie, standing, inviting the Earl of Shrewsbury, who is seated on his left, to perform the ceremony. The premises were originally built for the Cheadle Savings Bank in 1819.

The demolition, in 1956, of the building which had been used as Cheadle fire station from 1919 to 1955. Prior to 1919 the building had been stables for The Royal Oak Hotel.

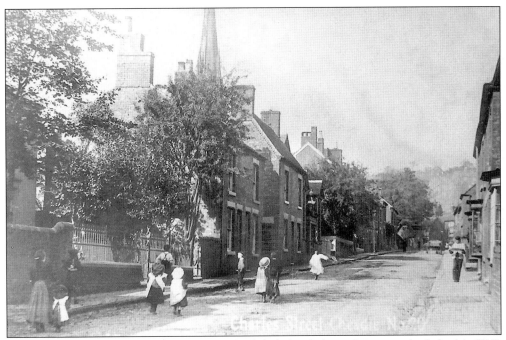

Charles Street in 1907. The building on the left, behind the railings, was built by Mr W.S. Allen in 1873 as a house for the assistant minister of the Methodist church. This building, now extended, is currently the Cheadle Social Club.

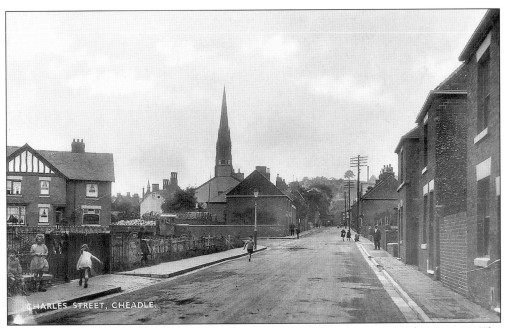

A 1940s view of Charles Street, showing a gas lamp at the junction with The Avenue. The chimney and works of the Cheadle Water Works can be seen on the far horizon, to the right of the telegraph pole.

The Times filling station in the 1930s. Mr Percy Emery, shown in the photograph, opened the filling station on Tean Road in the early 1920s. He originally purchased the petrol and oil from 'Russian Oil Products' and over the years the fuel has been supplied by a number of different companies. It is currently owned and supplied by Texaco.

Dr E. MacKenzie, Chairman of Cheadle Parish Council, opening the shelter on the Cheadle Recreation Ground, Tean Road, in 1934.

An aerial view of the County Council Schools in Cheadle, showing, in the foreground, the Senior School, built in 1931, later known as the MacKenzie School. To the right of it is the infants and primary school which was built in 1913. The roads that can be seen are Tean Road, Plant Street, Ashbourne Road, Tape Street, Charles Street and The Avenue. The new telephone exchange was built on the open area adjacent to The Avenue in 1964.

The Keates family, boot and shoe makers, opened their first shop in High Street in 1828. The business moved to Chapel Street in the early 1890s. This photograph, taken in 1898, shows Mr J.C. Keates, standing in the doorway, with John Wood and Jack Shaw. This shop closed in the 1960s.

The Grange, in Rakeway Road, was built in 1493. It had seven family rooms, utility rooms and an oak spiral staircase. It was demolished in 1966.

Acknowledgements

To Chris Mason of Tempus Publishing for his invitation to compile this collection of photographs. My thanks to all the people who have kindly loaned me photographs and documents for this selection:

Mesdames M. Bennett, A. Billings, N. Chell, C. Chester, N. Farmer, L. Hall, G. Lees, M. McCreedy, J. Plant and B. Sleigh. Messrs G. Beaman, R. Cartwright, A. Gilbert, B. Jeuda, K.C. Lovatt, R. Shaw, R.H. Smith, R.C. Taylor, D. Wardle and J. Wardle.

Thanks also go to: Campbells Photographers of Cheadle, Mr J. Taylor, *Leek Post and Times* and *Cheadle Post and Times* and other photographers of the area and to all those people who have kindly given information about the photographs.

I also thank my son, Ian, for editing and proofreading.